PLAN SAFE TRAVEL
SOLO

ALEX STARR

Clink
Street

London | New York

Published by Clink Street Publishing 2020

Copyright © 2020

First edition.

ISBN:

*For my parents, and for all the people
who make me feel alive again.*

I travel solo but you shape my journey.

'Plan Safe Travel' was written prior to the Covid-19 epidemic. Covid-19 should now also be considered when planning your trip. Ensure you:

- read the small print of health and travel insurance
- study entry and exit requirements of different countries
- save for unexpected financial extras.

Remember that you must feel comfortable with all your travel choices.

Happy planning!

INTRODUCTION

'Wait, you do that alone?'

No, I do it 'solo'. I choose to be alone or with strangers or with friends. I choose to travel my way.

A lack of time, money or confidence. Safety concerns. Dreading loneliness. The reasons not to go away are endless. But the pipedream lives on, so how do you make it a reality?

Consider the word 'alone'. Connotations of isolation and vulnerability dominate. Now, change this to the term 'solo'. It seems more neutral, correct? Suddenly, travelling seems less frightening and overwhelming. A 'solo' trip sounds empowering – although this is an individual journey, there is a choice to meet people along the way. Lifelong friendships can be forged and arise from the most surprising situations, yet opportunities are built in only with your permission. 'Alone' time can now be enjoyed, as there is a shift in perspective to it being desired and craved.

Nowadays, it is always easy to be surrounded by your own community too. Technology allows us to rarely feel cut off. With Wi-Fi increasingly ever-present in this world, friends and family provide support across long distances and rather than leaving them behind, they accompany you.

I have always loved travelling

For many years, I suppressed my passion and submitted to the pressures of society. But eight years of teaching high school English wore away enthusiasm, confidence and ambition. I was stuck in a rut. Confined by systems and norms, life was meaningless, lacked purpose and fulfilment. I'd turned 31 and realised that I was simply existing, not living. Ambivalence was ruling. An ambitious goal of travelling the world was born. It seemed daunting and unachievable, but stubborn and determined, my mind was set. I quit my career, sold my flat and set off...

Four years later, and life is my own: I have volunteered, travelled and lived abroad. It is my birthday and I am in Papua New Guinea, receiving an embrace from the tribal chief. It must be my fiftieth, sixtieth, seventieth country: I never count. Whilst others gloat of their adventures, social media popularity disinterests me. Instead, I pride myself on the view that greets me daily in the mirror. It happens to look ten years younger now – quite the bonus – but, more vitally, it is of a fulfilled, relaxed, smiley person.

This is not a book of memoirs or an autobiography

Over the years, I have made mistakes and met many vulnerable travellers who have encountered dangerous situations. Hindsight has led me to this moment. Whilst online forums, destination books and apps exist, until now, there has been no real emphasis placed on the early planning stages.

I aim to help you design your own safe adventure

We all are entirely unique. Our demands and expected outcomes of heading abroad are different. Booking a flight is easy, but lack of research leads to vulnerability. Naivety is our enemy; knowledge empowers and provides security.

This book guides you in understanding how to travel your way by providing a path through the decision-making process. Some questions are thought-provoking and difficult to answer, only raising more concerns. But considered trip design allows for greater confidence; deliberate and carefully selected decisions provide comfort, as you have a plan to avoid significant danger. This reassurance is liberating, as there is less distraction, anxiety and hesitancy. Although impossible to guarantee safety, instead being streetwise and enjoying the moment are your main priorities.

Even with a detailed itinerary, travelling can sometimes be unpredictable and through no fault of our own, inconvenient events occur, such as a delayed flight or a natural disaster.

As perfection is unachievable, we must therefore plan to ADAPT:

ASSESS Question your own situation alongside the country's present climate

DESIGN Answer by creating the outline to a trip

ABSORB Reflect on decisions

PREPARE Organise practically and mentally

TRAVEL Undertake the trip of your dreams safely!

With educated decisions come educated risks

Remember, never underestimate your own strength. Solo travelling takes bravery, so no matter the situation:

1. **TRUST YOUR JUDGEMENT** – instinct and gut feeling should lead all decision making. If it feels wrong, then it is. No explanation or justification is required.
2. **BE DECISIVE** – dithering leads to disorganisation and missed opportunities.
3. **APPRECIATE EVERY MOMENT.**

Plan safe travels everyone and enjoy your trip.
Alex

ASSESS

There are so many desirable destinations and travel options that establishing a starting point can feel complex. A good place to begin is:

WHAT DO YOU NEED OUT OF THE TRIP AND WHAT CAN DESTINATIONS OFFER?

I am inspired by the possibilities of who I can become and what I can achieve. It is empowering, enlightening and energising.

But most travellers rarely consider this assessment stage. Instead, having booked the flight, they then begin studying a guidebook. This is the wrong order, as you should read up on destination before paying out any money.

Two major components need researching:

1. **PERSONAL CONTEXT**
2. **THE COUNTRY'S CONTEXT: CURRENT CLIMATE**

Context is a current situation or state. These circumstances continually change, whether they are emotional, physical, political, economically or mental.

The key to unlocking the safe travel experience is accurately assessing how your own self, in this present moment, relates to the country of choice.

I. PERSONAL CONTEXT

For many, travelling is about 'finding yourself'. This theory holds one major flaw: you must understand your own needs before designing a travel plan. Of course, experiences like trekking around Nepal will teach new things, but the root of who you are will not have changed.

WHAT AFFECTS PERSONAL CONTEXT?

Budget
Unfortunately, money confines us. Plenty of people earn a wage remotely or abroad but usually, when booking a trip, there is a financial bottom line. Money is needed for travelling. Saving and saving and saving will help, but this still leads to an end number that cannot be surpassed. This figure should stand proud in your head, and in your bank account.

Crucially, I retain an 'excess budget' in my account. This is a hidden back-up that I am reluctant to spend. So many travellers state that they 'have no money'; however, travelling intelligently means possessing the finances to return home in any situation. Exhausting all my money is of no interest to me, feeling safe is. The excess budget is not for spending frivolously; it is a fund for emergencies.

How much should it be? Well, I need reassurance that I can always buy a ticket home, at any moment. The reality is that I dip into it only once or twice per trip. I often aim to catch a local bus from the airport to my accommodation but the plane delay of eight hours means that the arrival time is now 2 am and a more expensive, private taxi is a better idea. The excess budget is the 'trust my judgement' money that provides an alternative option in an otherwise uncomfortable situation. It is not a luxury, but a necessity, no matter the budget of the trip.

Capability

Travelling is frequently seen as a way of pushing ourselves, both physically or mentally, but who are you to begin with? Who do you want to become? What are you prepared to endure to get there? Understanding your own limitations is important. Everyone around you can judge and provide their opinions, but accountability sits with you alone. It is you who must live with the decisions.

A. **PHYSICAL CAPABILITY** lies with outer strength. What is your body capable of achieving?

I accept that sitting in a jeep in Namibia waiting to see lions in the wild for ten hours straight will never appeal to me because I get backache and stiff joints. You too may never want to sit in one spot for more than a couple of hours, instead desiring to cycle trails or run marathons every day. Physical demands, including travel time and carrying backpacks, need to be considered. The longer the trip, the fitter the body becomes, but travelling is exhausting and it is easy to run out of steam.

Be careful not to underestimate the body's potential either. Last year, I met a couple who travel the world continuously, having sold their entire life in the States. She is in a wheelchair and her supposed restraints rightly fail to prevent her enjoyment of the world. As a couple, they continually discuss all decisions related to physicality.

A. **MENTAL CAPABILITY** lies with inner strength. What is your mind capable of achieving?

Travelling solo can be tough, as nobody else looks after you. How hard are you willing to push yourself? In 2016, I visited Vietnam entirely independently. Alone and inexperienced, I felt vulnerable and exposed. I had neglected to assess my mental strength; at that time, I was too weak for this travel style. I should have identified this more clearly but naivety and determination had prevailed over sense.

Again, the mind can be underestimated – strength grows and, inevitably, travellers become more empowered and self-assured by the end of a trip.

Time

Time can be short and on so many occasions, we all wish we had more of it. Sometimes, we require less. Deadlines and time scales are ever-present; a return date is probably already glued into your diary. This makes it important to consider pace. The less familiar the culture and language, the more energy a trip consumes. Would you rather spend significant time in one country, allowing for deeper understanding of a culture and society, or touch on many destinations just acquiring a taste of the region?

Outcome

What achievements do you want to accomplish from this trip? Are they related to people, culture, history, geography or yourself? Do you want to detach from society and feel a sense of remoteness?

Success criteria can be set from the start – perhaps it is a desire to enjoy local cuisine or to visit the Taj Mahal due its history and splendour. We seldom sit and contemplate what we want to achieve. On many occasions, it is merely that a country is appealing, or, more likely, is in fashion. A feature in a recent newspaper article or social media post makes us believe we want to go – and now! Just because you have a clear destination in mind, doesn't mean it is the right one; there are hundreds of other alternatives that may be more fulfilling.

Typically, the best and most memorable experiences are unexpected, whether it be the kindness of a stranger or a profound conversation. Being open to these opportunities enhances enjoyment. Jordan, 2018. I spilt my heart to a complete stranger and received incredible support. Decisions made that day continue to affect me and our friendship remains strong, despite the distance between us.

Consider what you desire from the trip and then be entirely surprised by the unforeseen bonus outcomes that occur alongside.

Comfort Level

What is the standard of accommodation, transfers and transportation that you expect on this trip?

A. ACCOMMODATION

When travelling, society expects a norm. Stereotypically, 18-year-olds should share a dorm in an underwhelming youth hostel, whilst 60-year-olds should stay in a 4 or 5* hotel. In 2016, I was expected to revert back to a backpacker lifestyle, despite having been a professional and home-owner for many years. I was effectively unemployed and therefore should save every penny on accommodation.

I have a major issue with the word 'should'.

The strength of a solo traveller is underestimated. People continually pressurise you and feel empowered to judge, insult or question your decisions because they still see you as 'alone'. As a 35-year-old woman, a cruise ship 'should' absolutely not be my preferred accommodation, but it has been in the past and will continue to be in the future, if it suits my assessment. Resilience builds over time, and now I ignore the expectation that I must justify myself to complete strangers who ask, 'how can you afford to travel this way?'

Ultimately, I select accommodation that makes me feel less vulnerable.

Once you have established your comfort level, never compromise. Instead, treat yourself by increasing the standard occasionally.

HOSTELS are associated with a backpacker lifestyle because they are the cheapest form of accommodation. Dorms are either single sex or mixed, but there are also private rooms.

Single sex dorms and private rooms are more expensive, but again, money is not the priority. In a mixed dorm, privacy can feel invaded. Common fears include being sexually assaulted or being accused of violating others. The trust expected of roommates is extremely high.

Although luggage is safer in private rooms, meeting like-minded people is more probable in a dorm. Exploring sights in the evening then happens together; in a more precarious area, this is something that staying individually might forfeit.

In some cultures, solo female travelling is frowned upon. Male travel companions, met in a mixed dorm, become valuable bodyguards against unwanted attention (add a faux engagement ring for extra effect), as a 'couple' is more widely accepted. Despite the striving for equality in Western society, safety means respecting, acknowledging and adhering to different cultural norms, not critiquing them.

HOTELS offer private rooms. The additional expense buys the home luxuries of a comfy bed, en-suite bathroom, television and possibly even a breakfast. Lock the door and there is a feeling of security, although it can feel a little isolating.

HOUSESITTING is the latest craze, particularly popular in Australasia. Due to the more isolated geographical position of the continent, many people venture abroad for several weeks. Websites connect those requiring accommodation with those going on vacation. Although there is small subscription fee, the stay is then free. Precise dates are set by the home owner, and there is normally a pet to look after. After arrival, it is difficult to cancel, so be prepared to commit.

APARTMENTS provide much welcome independence – useful when there's a bag of laundry or a sudden desire to make toast! A private apartment costs more, but rooms within shared spaces are available. Renting from strangers can be challenging, especially when travelling solo. My friend told me that in the middle of the night, she awoke to find her host standing in the doorway watching her, so check that there is a lock on the bedroom door and a safe in the room.

It is also worth discussing lifestyle choices before booking, as people inhabit spaces differently. Some companies are unsympathetic with a delayed arrival time and there is rarely storage for luggage after checkout.

Finally, **CRUISE SHIPS** are a more luxurious option: a high standard hotel floating on water, with transportation, food and drink all included in one price. A cashless system on board means that you don't even need to carry money around.

A.   TRANSFERS AND TRANSPORTATION

A TRANSFER is the method of travelling between accommodation and an airport/station in a new destination. Public transportation is usually available. Generally, a bus route is longer and less direct than the metro/underground. Private transfers are more expensive but at least can be pre-booked before leaving home. Strangers may approach you, offering cheap options, but always use a reputable taxi company.

TRANSPORTATION is the method of travelling between destinations. Some journeys span long distances. Night buses/trains can be uncomfortable but they ensure no hours of daylight are wasted, as departure times are late and arrival times are early. The alternative is flying, which is more comfortable but also more money.

Before progressing any further, check your passport. Many countries now require several blank pages inside. There are also certain stipulations about the expiry date, as entry can be refused if validity is less than six months. So, is there enough time and space left?

TASK

Now reflect on your personal context.
Use the boxes below to make notes.

2. THE COUNTRY'S CONTEXT: CURRENT CLIMATE

 Every destination has a current climate. Researching the important issues and possible foibles of a country really assists with trip design and preparation.

TASK

Answer the following questions:

1. What is the political situation?
2. What is the official religion?
3. What is the economic situation? What does £20 buy? Is it easy to exchange money?
4. What is the attitude towards women?
5. What is the attitude towards Westerners?
6. What is the attitude towards solo travellers?
7. What is the official government advice on travelling to this destination?
8. What events and issues have been recently reported in the news and on social media?
9. How much is a night in your accommodation of choice?
10. What are the weather conditions on a month by month basis?
11. What language is spoken? Is the script the same as English?

12. What visas are required? How easy are they to access and how much do they cost?
13. Are there any current health scares in the region?
14. How popular is the destination with tourists? Is there a set route for tourists to follow?
15. What are the cultural highlights of the country? Consider history, geography, food, culture.
16. What scams have occurred recently in this destination?

This information continually changes. Hundreds of travel blogs exist based on personal experience alone. They can be misleading, unhelpful and out-of-date. Of course, they advise, assist and inspire but official records are key to fact finding. Every government has a website dedicated to travel advice and information is categorised by country. Search and study each option carefully.

This is your experience and nobody else's; information is required that can be completely relied upon. A friend who visited ten years ago will casually discuss their experience but this does not mean the stories are relevant, or accurate anymore.

The answers must be from this year and this month.

Many consider a more popular destination safer. True, as there is security in numbers, but false because methods of exploiting the more economically rich Western tourist have been refined and developed over time.

Whilst in Vietnam, I discovered the 'market trap'. For your first purchase, the vendor provides a secretly 'coded' coloured bag, which is assigned based on your level of bartering. The colour becomes an advertisement of your monetary status and whether others can hike their prices up. Scams like these are difficult to learn before reaching a destination but search engines highlight some of the most popular.

HOW DOES THE COUNTRY FIT AROUND YOUR NEEDS?

Both the current climate of a country and your personal context are fixed. They are unable to change.

Consider whether a country can fulfil all your needs, without compromise. Ignoring your specific requirements will only lead to difficulties.

This I learnt from experience. I once risked my safety because I failed to act on research collated.

In 2017, I volunteered in Costa Rica. The opportunity to work in a specially designed project for the government (aiming to improve the standard of English teaching in the region) was just too tempting. Recent newspaper reports had already informed me that attacks on locals were high. Instead of dismissing the experience, I pushed on and booked, thinking I knew better. At 8 am, on a bright, sunny day, a man stepped out from behind me. His intentions were unclear – rape, mugging, kidnap, murder – I still dread to consider the possibilities. Women in Costa Rica do not fight back. I did: I screamed; I kicked; I swore; I shouted; I fought. I ended up in hospital – thankfully, only with whiplash. For my volunteer coordinator, host and colleagues surprise only lay in the fact that I had never experienced this before in my own country. They accept violence on locals as their norm.

The truth is that I should never have accepted the placement because I knew not to become a local. The solo traveller is not invincible and I should have trusted my original assessment.

TASK

Use the following table to analyse whether
the country meets all your needs.

Myself		Country		How does the country fit around your needs?
What is my budget? What is my excess budget?		1. What is the political situation?		Can I see and experience everything for my budget?
		2. What is the official religion?		
		3. What is the economic situation? What does £20 buy? Is it easy to exchange money?		
		4. What is the attitude towards women?		
What are my physical capabilities? What are my mental capabilities? What do I want to achieve?		5. What is the attitude towards Westerners?		Will this trip test my limits? Will this trip push me too far? Have I read anything that indicates that I should not be going?
		6. What is the attitude towards solo travellers?		
		7. What is the official government advice about travelling to this destination?		
		8. What events and issues have recently been reported in newspapers and on social media?		
How long do I have to travel?	+	9. How much is a night in your accommodation of choice?	=	Do I have enough time? Do I have too much time? Will I be able to do each destination justice?
		10. What are the weather conditions on a month by month basis?		
		11. What language is spoken? Is the script the same as English?		
What am I hoping to achieve from this trip?		12. What visas are required? How easy are they to access and how much do they cost?		Does this trip fulfil all of my requirements? Can I achieve exactly what I desire? Will I feel safe?
		13. Are there any current health scares in the region?		
		14. How popular is the destination with tourists? Is there a set route that tourists follow?		
What level of comfort do I demand from the trip?		15. What are the cultural highlights of the country? Consider history, geography, food, culture.		Is the level of comfort I want achievable?
		16. What scams have occurred recently in this destination?		

Life is full of compromises. However, these must not occur during the assessment stage. The ultimate question is: should I be travelling to this country? Only with a confident and assured 'yes' should trip design start. The 'how' now needs defining.

DESIGN

Designing a trip is now much easier because your assessment will have already narrowed down some options. Generally, a plan is formulated in our minds from the very beginning. We are headstrong; this is a prerequisite for being a solo traveller. However, sometimes our preconceived ideas are incorrect. Doggedly determined, ploughing on with booking anything and everything often leads to regret after a few days, weeks or months on the road.

Instead, for now, suppress the craving for spontaneity and follow the correct path:

STEP 1:
DECIDE ON A TRAVEL STYLE

STEP 2:
DESIGN THE TRIP OUTLINE

STEP 3:
DESIGN THE FINER-DETAIL ELEMENTS

STEP 1: DECIDE ON A TRAVEL STYLE

Most travellers are unaware that they have a choice of travel styles. These are:

- INDEPENDENT
- ORGANISED TRIP
- VOLUNTEERING
- WORK

INDEPENDENT

People automatically assume travelling means being 'independent'. From booking a flight to a night bus journey to a hostel bedroom, this style means designing and completing the trip by yourself. This either scares or inspires you.

There is an overwhelming choice of accommodation, transportation and activities on the internet: the list is endless – as are the opinions and the reviews.

The biggest decision associated with travelling independently is the quantity you want to book before leaving home. This can be every miniscule detail to actually very little. There is a relationship between organisation and budget though: the more planned, the better control you have over money. In spite of this, many travellers are entirely spontaneous. They leave on a departing flight, with their name signed against nothing else. There is a fine line between bravery and foolishness. It is worth booking that first hostel or hotel. Arriving entirely jetlagged, disorientated and emotional (being at the start of your physical and mental journey), new cultures are overwhelming. Book a more luxurious room than normal for your arrival city, as you will need time to process change.

ORGANISED TRIPS

This travel style consists of joining a group of strangers and embarking on a tour together with a local leader. Usually, the pre-paid price includes accommodation and transportation, amongst other extras. Organised trips differ immensely in size and price but they can be an ideal way of maintaining a grip on your budget. Some more locally based companies unfortunately demand a single supplement.

Travelling as a community can be a great way to meet people, although you are still responsible for your own safety. The leader removes the burden of booking buses, trains, car journeys, hotels, hostels and an array of other details. However, fundamentally, they are not a babysitting service. Free to roam the streets of Lima or experience the local salsa club in Santiago, not every minute of the day will be accompanied – good news if you do not like feeling claustrophobic.

Each tour provides detailed trip notes. To avoid unexpected surprises, these need to be studied carefully. Look closely at journey times between destinations, as there can be very long days.

Many argue this travel style is cost ineffective, as the same route can normally be completed independently for less money. However, it depends where value lies. With less responsibility for organising practicalities, time is more effectively used. There is also no price on safety. At 22, I spent three months travelling from Brazil to Peru. Inexperienced and insecure, I was not ready to complete an adventure independently, as flying on a plane without family seemed a challenge. An organised trip increased my confidence and I was able to enjoy all the destinations.

You will fly into the starting point alone. Are you comfortable with this? On one occasion, I asked an operator whether she would arrive in Managua alone. Her response was a firm 'no', yet her company still offered this tour. I immediately rejected the option but if I had not asked the question, would she have sold it to me anyway?

Search engines produce hundreds of organised trip options and it is vital to check review sites. For reputable companies, begin by visiting a travel agent.

So, what qualifies as an organised tour? If several aspects of a trip are planned for you, then it is organised. For me, this includes cruising. Ten years ago, I would never have considered this travel style, mostly because I was unaware of the cheap deals (even with a single supplement). Now, I am forever searching – and sailing.

In 2016, I wanted to travel around Indonesia. I had found two options: a ten-day cruise and a conventional, overland, organised tour. The itineraries were the same. The more expensive option required three different boat trips to-and-from the mainland to Komodo Island, Bali and Lombok. The cheaper option demanded that I stayed in 5* luxury. It was a no-brainer and I booked the cruise.

Dropping my valuables inside the cabin was a huge relief, as I had been travelling independently for several weeks beforehand. I realised that I was exhausted and I was able to recuperate completely in a safe environment. At ports, I disembarked alone or sometimes paid for a ship tour. Although the clientele is typically more mature, everyone on board has the same outlook, which is to experience new places and have fun.

VOLUNTEERING

Many travellers want to make a difference. The volunteering sector provides thousands of opportunities, from building hospitals to teaching English.

Local, worldwide and independent companies can be found online. Your decisions include the length, work and country. Finding the perfect option is difficult, as they all offer unique experiences. Usually, the traveller pays a fee, so the project must fulfil all requirements and be worth the commitment. Some companies retain this profit for themselves, whilst others use the money to improve the lives of locals.

A varying amount of your daytime and evening activities are organised. As a project aims for improvement, you will be living in a more undesirable location, so you may feel unsafe independently exploring. With research, there can be the perfect opportunity, but it is important to understand the region and expectations before signing up.

The commitment time ranges from a week to six months. Volunteering is therefore an opportunity to remain in one location, so a much deeper connection is made with the local community.

WORK

From visas to employment rights to tax payments, working abroad is complicated and challenging.

Teaching English abroad, via obtaining a TEFL certificate, is a popular way of remaining in one country whilst earning an income. From being a barman to a chalet assistant, the opportunities are endless. Many companies advertise vacancies online and either you secure a position before leaving home or you relocate without employment. No job means no money, so your excess budget must be high.

Visas cost money and terms and conditions only permit a traveller to work for the same company for a set number of months. Therefore, although you are committing to a country for a longer time period, expect some instability.

TASK

Use the flow chart below to decipher your most suited travel style for this trip.

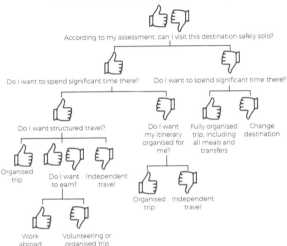

Social media creates the image of an idyllic travel life-style; however, it is a perceived reality. Their purpose is to increase popularity and the difficulties encountered are generally not represented. Although we may have firm ideas that we want to travel completely inde-pendently, sometimes other travel styles meet our requirements better.

We have to learn to adapt our expectation, so as to not compromise on safety.

STEP 2: DESIGN THE OUTLINE

The itinerary now needs designing. Eventually, every element of the trip must be organised but for now, the current priorities are the overview: the route, flights and some accommodation. Future decisions include transfers, transportation, day-to-day content and food and drink, but this order depends on travel style.

WHO CAN HELP WITH TRIP DESIGN?

Element	Traveller	Travel Agent	Organised Trip or Volunteering Project	Workplace
Route	✓	✓	✓	X
Flights	✓	✓	✓	X
Accommodation	✓	✓	✓	X (Sometimes)
Transportation	✓	✓	✓	X (Sometimes)
Transfers	✓	✓	✓ Airport transfers can be extra.	X (Sometimes)
Day activities	✓	✓	X Each day is different	X (Sometimes)
Food and drink	✓	X	✓⇨X Each day is different	X (Sometimes)

Key

Overview elements

Finer-detail elements

Put simply, you have two major choices: either use a travel agent or search for every element yourself on the internet.

Reputable travel agents, particularly for gap years, have existed on the high street for decades. There is a misconception that they are purely aimed at post-university students – any person who wants assistance can use them.

Travel agents are knowledgeable professionals, who have a wealth of experience and contacts. Their advice is useful. They can relieve pressure, particularly of organisation, as they already collaborate with visa companies, organised trip companies and airlines. Most purchases are ATOL or ABTA protected, which means you will never be stranded abroad. This support can be invaluable, especially in unexpected situations. Nobody could have predicted New Zealand's worst winter weather on record. Everyone else was trapped, but my travel agent found me the only flight out of Christchurch on that blizzardous day.

But all companies hold an agenda: to sell you a product. Their focus is on offering you the cheapest deal. With welfare being your number one priority, spend time finding the best option, not just the one that saves the most money.

Ownership comes entirely from you, the traveller.

They cannot be expected to understand your requirements unless you communicate them. Even selecting the right organised trip or project can be challenging – searching can take weeks. Leading the conversations is fundamental, without being swayed by sales techniques, as you will be flying out of your local airport alone.

ROUTES

Determine how many days are appropriate for each destination. The assessment stage will have advised on key recommendations. Even if you plan to travel independently, it is worth ordering or accessing organised trip brochures because they highlight itineraries, popular routes and a suggested number of days for each location. Guidebooks, the internet, personal and professional recommendations are all useful as well.

FLIGHTS

Travel agents sell around-the-world flights. Major airlines are part of alliances. Each one usually offers a package that includes three to five major city stops in different continents, for a ticket price. Cost effective and flexible, this option allows for travelling across a larger number of destinations for a longer timescale. If finding flights independently, by slightly adjusting arrival and departure dates, you might discover better deals. Return flights are generally better value for money than a one-way ticket.

ACCOMMODATION

Typically, it is difficult to find the perfect hotel, hostel or apartment because there is a conflict between standard and location. Accommodation around bus or train stations is cheaper because these areas are usually the most precarious. There is therefore merit in checking a city's transportation links; staying slightly further away from the main attractions means getting more for your money, even after adding the costs of metro/ underground tickets. If your travel style is an organised trip, the tour will begin in a specific hotel, so purchase the pre-tour accommodation (and the transfer).

When designing the outline elements, record each new option, labelling the source. Using a table, include the website, company, contact details and cancellation conditions.

Example:

Location	Style of Travel	Days Required	Dates	Cost
Lima	Independent	3?	11th March	Further research required
Inca Trail and Cusco	Group tour	7	14th/15th March approx.	£599 ('An Inca Trail to Remember') or £487 ('Cusco and Beyond'). Non-refundable.
Buenos Aires	Independent	5	21st/22nd March – 27th March	Further research required.
Buenos Aires	Independent	0 – direct flight home	27th/28th March	£746 (return flight Gatwick – Lima and Buenos Aires – Gatwick). Denise 0208****** Ext no: 786. Non-refundable

Ensure that the outline figures remain well within your budget. Listing all options together helps with debating alternatives later.

Be aware: the outline requires large pay-outs but the finer-detail elements combined all add up to a significant amount of money.

Book nothing yet.

STEP 3: DESIGN THE FINER-DETAIL ELEMENTS

Some people hold the carefree approach that they should only design the basic outline of a trip, as the unpredictability of travelling creates excitement. Undoubtably, there is a relationship between spontaneity and design, as the more you research, the less spontaneity is possible:

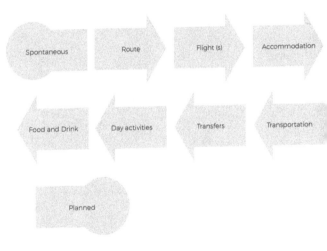

However, a responsible and safe solo-traveller considers some of the finer-detail elements.

TRANSPORTATION AND TRANSFERS

Your comfort level assessment should have determined your transportation and transfer choices. Now, use search engines to find the right option.

- **What is the availability of transportation from one destination to another?** The departure/arrival time and cost of a train, bus or plane departure might affect the number of days that you spend in a location.
- **What is the best method of reaching accommodation?** On arrival, it is the unfamiliarity of a new destination that makes you vulnerable.

DAY ACTIVITIES/FOOD AND DRINK

It is frustrating wasting precious time queuing. You also do not want to miss opportunities that could have been easily organised in advance.

- **What entrance tickets can be pre-booked?**
- **Do you want to visit any specific restaurants, events or productions?**

For each finer-detail element, record all possible options.

Example:

Destination: Malaysia						
Destination	Transportation	Accommodation	Day Activities	Food and drink	Other experiences	Notes
Kuala Lumpur 10th – 15th October	Monorail from the airport.	The View Hotel, Petronas Towers	No pre-booking needed	Read in guide book that food is amazing. Eat a variety!	Batu Caves?	Muslim country – how conservative should clothing be?
Malacca 15th– 16h October	KL-Malacca = easy to organise in KL. Unsure which form of transportation is best.	Lots of hotels, no need to decide	No pre-booking needed	Asian food supposed to be outstanding		
Penang 16th – 20th October	Cheap flights. Loads. Book in KL	Lots of hotels, no need to decide	Cooking class at Sage Hotel	Unsure, as not read about it.	Snorkelling	

Aim to secure and pre-pay before leaving home.

This table effectively becomes your itinerary and 'to-do' list combined. It can also be updated with confirmation and reference numbers at a later date.

The search for options begins now, as designing elements eventually leads to booking.

You might argue that you don't want to pre-book everything. Nonetheless, this table is a way of maintaining control, helping you to feel grounded and relaxed, as it reminds you of the tasks that still need organising.

Remember though that for some destinations, reserving accommodation early is a necessity, as there may only be one hostel available, due to its remote location or a famous local event occurring. For many cities, money is a leading factor, as rooms can become very expensive.

To me, value is using every moment to experience a destination, not squandering precious afternoons designing or booking. Although my compromise is my flexibility, I would still rather complete everything at home, so that spare time away can be used to revitalise and re-energise after exhausting days.

Design the finer-detail elements now because a clear, focused mind always results in a more confident attitude and approach.

Remember: book nothing yet.

TASK

What is the right level of trip design for you?

Circle your preferences based on what you want to design before leaving home.

Flights?	Yes	Some	No
Accommodation	Yes	Some	No
Transfers & transportation?	Yes	Some	No
Day activities?	Yes	Some	No
Food and drink?	Yes	Some	No

Circle your preferences based on what you want to book before leaving home.

Flights?	Yes	Some	No
Accommodation	Yes	Some	No
Transfers & transportation?	Yes	Some	No
Day activities?	Yes	Some	No
Food and drink?	Yes	Some	No

ABSORB

The shortest chapter but the longest pause; this is the chance to absorb the reality of the trip, before booking.

People might encourage an impulsive 'just go for it' attitude. You will probably want to confirm every detail immediately, before losing courage. Yes, take risks. Yes, be impulsive. Yes, be open to new, exciting opportunities.

But you need to feel secure that the trip designed is your best choice and this needs a moment of reflection.

There may be pressure to grab opportunities with deadlines on deals for flights or accommodation. However, other travel options will present themselves whereas thinking time does not. In the past, with a gung-ho approach, I have launched full throttle into handing over vast amounts of money. I regret nothing but now possess the hindsight that I should have considered the enormity of my decisions more.

SO, WHAT NEEDS ABSORBING?

TASK

Before booking, the answers to the following
questions must be 'yes'. Tick as completed.

OVERALL FEELINGS

Is this trip worthwhile?

This money will never re-enter your bank account.
Hours, weeks, years of hard work, all gone is one
payment. We all value money differently. Value
might be spending thousands on the comfort of
first-class plane tickets or it might be stretching the
equivalent over several months. Are you happy to
spend such a large amount on the itinerary created? There is no shame in withdrawing and there
is no justification required.

Many years ago, I almost signed up for a three-week
Morocco trip. It felt wrong. Gut instinct and intuition
prevented me from paying out anything. I didn't go.
I still do not regret it. However, I do regret the time I
paid in full for a trip to South Africa without reading
the small print. The organised tour got cancelled. The
consequence: a flight to Johannesburg with no plans.

I didn't go there either. I lost all my money because I failed to read the terms and conditions carefully.

Are you pushing yourself physically and mentally the right amount?

The design must match your personal assessment. Planning relaxation time is key, no matter the time period that you are away. Even if the trip is only two weeks, being on the go and looking after yourself is exhausting; it should not be underestimated. Continually watching belongings, people and money is shattering. There need to be moments where the pressure is relieved. For a few days, sit on a beach or book a private, more luxurious room, especially if you are visiting locations where money stretches further. Switching off completely recuperates the body and mind, so design these moments for a physical and mental break.

Do you have enough time to prepare?

Without the yellow fever certificate, it is impossible to enter some countries. Without the India visa, it is impossible to visit India. This might all sound obvious. Then again, there is no point in booking anything if there is not enough time left to obtain all the entry requirements – save this trip for another occasion.

FINER-DETAILS FEELINGS

Are your flights and transportation decisions correct?

Try to arrive at your destination at a reasonable time, especially if contending with jetlag. Too early and the day is very long. Too late and the strange, unfamiliar city is already dark. On one occasion, I arrived in Tokyo at 8 am. Trying to stay awake all day was challenging, exhausting and disorientating. In these circumstances, I email the hotel to warn them that I desire an early check-in. At least then there is somewhere to rest and leave luggage.

It is much easier to arrive mid to late afternoon because the room is accessible. There is only a short window of daytime left – a useful few hours for orientating yourself and grabbing food, before heading to sleep early. Waking up the next day, you will feel more refreshed and a little less lost.

These rules apply to the departure time as well. If the flight doesn't leave until late evening, who will hold your baggage during the day? Most accom-modation provides a locked storage room for an extra fee. If the flight leaves in the early morning, how will you transfer to the airport? Is the area safe for reaching public transportation? Do the local buses even run that early?

Is the itinerary paced correctly?

A jam-packed itinerary leads to a sense of chaos and panic, caused by too much rushing around. Whilst you want to be eager and use time effectively, it is vital to remain calm and relaxed. It is always more advantageous to have slightly too many days in one location than too few.

Is your accommodation correct?

Like most people, I prefer deals, but, as a general rule, the phrase 'too good to be true' exists for a reason, so check review sites. On my first visit to Singapore, I'd booked a 4* hotel for under £90 per night. What the internet failed to report – or I hadn't researched – was that it happened to be beside a building site.

Are the companies reputable?

Be reassured that all travel agents use reputable companies and major flight companies are popular because they highly regarded. During trip design, you may have discovered other opportunities online, especially a cheap (usually domestic) flight with a more unknown airline. It is important to search for safety reports and act on the advice found. Check social media and review sites. Research the company's financial situation. Use recommendations where possible.

Will my itinerary lead to loneliness?

Being alone for too long leads to loneliness. It is best to pre-empt this from the beginning.

A good solution is a short tour. Too much time can be lost deciding what to see and how best to see it. For a fee, companies offer the all-inclusive hour, morning, afternoon or day out. In 2019, before I left home, I pre-booked one for over three months later. I knew that by Tasmania, I would be missing the company of the friends that I was due to stay with in Melbourne beforehand. My assessment also indicated that there would be no public transport to visit remote sights. Despite high cost, a ten-hour tour seemed a good decision and on reflection, it was one of the best I made for Australia. In a mini-bus, I saw nine of the most outstanding, stunning places, whilst enjoying the company of eight other strangers. I had avoided loneliness successfully.

Over-planning opportunities to meet people is also negative. Too many nights sleeping in a shared dorm makes you feel suffocated. This is because our sense of self rapidly grows whilst away. It is therefore crucial to build in the breathing space to reflect upon personal development. Without it, experiences become overwhelming and it is easy to become caught up in other people's bad decisions, as there is just no time to stop and question them.

HOW DO YOU KNOW WHEN YOU ARE READY TO BOOK?

There is doubt, nervousness, fear, exhilaration but a sense of clarity, certainty, comfort and contentment.

Turn back to the design stage checklists and tables. Begin by booking the overview and then methodically progress through the finer-details. Always pay on official booking platforms. Use a credit card for more protection.

Your dream is suddenly a reality and it is time to begin preparing.

PREPARE

Hurl items into a rucksack, and step onto a plane. Is jetting off abroad so simple? Anticipation building, the final steps towards making the trip a reality are exciting, if not, frustrating. It is time to begin preparing.

Being ready is not only related to packing – in fact, although this area is most commonly considered first, it should be organised last. Other practical steps need prioritising instead, such as injections and visas.

DOCUMENTATION

The **passport** is the most important document. Scan and print copies now. **Place a copy into both hand luggage and your suitcase/backpack, just in case the original is lost or stolen and leave another with a loved one at home.**

All **visas** cost money. You can apply independently or, for an additional small processing fee, through a travel agent/company. This option relieves stress from often challenging application forms. Prioritise visas, as your passport must be posted off too and it can take time to be returned. Some countries only require an electronic visa but always use official government websites: be careful of scams.

Insurance is compulsory and can be purchased for a single trip or an entire year. For some nations, healthcare is entirely private and the package includes travelling abroad. Europeans can still apply for a European Health Card, which provides free healthcare across the continent. But travel insurance also includes lost luggage and cancellations. There are many cheap plans available, but always read the small print, as protection needs to be a high enough value to cover all eventualities. **Put copies of the policy with the copies of your passport.**

In 2007, I ate a sandwich that had not been stored in the fridge: it was the last thing I ate for three weeks. Diagnosed with gastroenteritis, I was sick. Unable to carry my rucksack, thankfully, I was travelling on an organised trip, and had new friends to care for me. However, an 18-hour night bus from Buenos Aires to southern Argentina was looming. It seemed entirely unachievable, so I purchased a flight (from my excess budget), and re-joined the group the next day. By this time, I had paid out for hospital appointments and medication; insurance companies will not pay immediately, unless it is an emergency. **Bad experiences happen but keep all receipts, x-rays and paperwork** together, so that you can submit a claim on your return home.

Finally, print the full **itinerary** (with all booking references) and store it digitally. Several apps organise key documents but I tend to just place confirmations into a separate folder of my email. Provide a copy to close family members, just in case of emergency. Do not publicise precise booking details on social media.

To remain organised, store all documentation in a plastic wallet and then pack into hand luggage.

MONEY

Cash. Generally, the more converted, the better the rate, but this can result in too many notes and coins being in your wallet. It is a burden and pressure to continually protect money, so only change the minimum required. It is much easier to relax with funds safely in your bank account.

Nevertheless, too little is also dangerous. Always have enough to pay for a taxi, to provide an escape route in any situation. People say 'avoid exchanging currency at an airport' – true, as rates can be exploitative – but **travelling safely solo means entering a new country with cash in your wallet**. Last year, I converted money in Kuala Lumpur airport. I had been uncertain as to the cost of the taxi journey there. My hotel was relatively remote, so obtaining Singapore dollars any earlier had been impossible. Fundamentally, choosing to lose a few pounds was much more important than entering a new country penniless.

We no longer live in a cash centred society. With this, the travel money industry has developed and progressed too (thankfully the days of traveller's cheques are in the past). A plethora of **pre-paid travel money cards** are now available, with some storing up to seven currencies on one account. They function as a debit card, without further additional charges, and can be cancelled, if stolen. Currency is effortlessly and securely loaded through an app or website, ready for using either immediately or at a future date. This is particularly beneficial in challenging economic times. In March 2019, the original Brexit deadline led me to pre-empt a weak pound, so in December 2018, I invested early in Canadian dollars. It was May 2019 before I arrived in Vancouver, but I had saved money by converting months in advance.

Importantly, read the terms and conditions carefully and leave login details with a loved one, so that they can add funds on your behalf. My friend was already abroad when he realised that his card would only load in the UK (his home country); he had to rely on his **debit card** instead and the withdrawals cost an exorbitant amount. Consequently, it is also worth informing your bank that you will be heading away, as sometimes they block your account if they suspect unusual activity.

A **credit card** provides protection for the purchaser. I remember once an airline processed payment for a flight twice. It was the credit card company that fought for my reimbursement.

Years ago, I increased my possible maximum limit. Although I never even intend on using the account abroad, I now have more options in the unwelcome case of a real emergency, imminent danger or health situation. I also clear my entire bill before travelling, so I know the exact figure available in my current account. This helps to maintain a more stable expenditure, as there are no surprise outgoings.

Whilst away, lock all credit and debit cards in the safe. You only need the pre-paid travel card and some cash during the day. Never use ATM machines in the evening and always try to withdraw money inside a bank building.

HEALTH

A.   PHYSICAL HEALTH

How can the experts help me to prepare?

Always visit a medical professional before embarking on a major trip abroad.

In the UK, most doctor surgeries employ a travel nurse. Advice is personalised, so take your itinerary with you. They provide many of the necessary **injections** immediately, although some are unavailable on the NHS and require payment. You will be directed to the nearest specialist clinic.

The travel nurse establishes whether the countries are affected by malaria. There are different types of **antimalarial** drugs that greatly contrast in price, but there is a correlation between side-effects and expense. Although money can be saved on cheaper options, it is not ideal to contend with sickness whilst away and a healthier body is a much safer option.

How can I prepare?

Purchasing medication is straightforward in developed countries, but consider which brands you use frequently at home, and take those with you, as strength and names may be unfamiliar. Travel first aid kits are sold on the high street, but over the years, I have created my own. In it I pack:

1. **PAIN RELIEF.** Paracetamol is ideal for general pain relief, but incredibly difficult to purchase outside of the UK.
2. **ANTI-INFLAMMATORY TABLETS.** Unfortunately, accidents occur. A short course reduces swelling.
3. **DIARRHOEA TABLETS.** Even for the most experienced traveller, diarrhoea is a common occurrence. Like all medication, do not overuse, but these tablets are handy for long journeys, when toilets are unavailable or unsanitary.
4. **REHYDRATION PACKS.** Dilute these simple-to-use sachets in a bottle of water. They restore some key vitamins, helping you to feel more re-vitalised, especially after diarrhoea or sickness.
5. **SCISSORS**
6. **ANTISEPTIC WIPES.** Buy the pre-packed, individually sealed wipes, as bottles spill. Clean all cuts and grazes.
7. **PLASTERS.** Look for a variety of sizes and shapes, so that you can protect any blister or cut.
8. **MOSQUITO REPELLENT SPRAY AND BRACELETS.** Medical professionals recommend at least 50% DEET, which is hard to purchase overseas.

9. **ANTIHISTAMINES**. Bites occur. Keep them controlled, to avoid infection.
10. **TRAVEL SICKNESS TABLETS AND BANDS**. Exhaustion leaves you feeling jaded and nauseous on long journeys.

Sexual liberation is often a part of the travelling experience. Always use protection, to prevent the contraction of STIs and HIV. Transmission also occurs through contaminated blood supply, so avoid manicures and pedicures, which are particularly tempting in Asia, as they are extremely cheap. The same hygiene rules fail to exist abroad, and one wrong cut of a cuticle from an unclean instrument could be more trouble than beautiful nails are ever worth!

B. MENTAL HEALTH

Mindfulness techniques are helpful, especially if you suffer from an anxious predisposition. As part of your preparation, learn how to cope with stressful, adrenaline fuelled situations. Remaining calm and slowing a panicked heartrate, even in difficult circumstances, is challenging. Decisions must be made quickly and overanalysing details leads to distraction. For me, there is a link between physical exercise and a calm mental state. To maintain control, every few weeks, I book a hotel with a gym or pool.

PACKING

A. LUGGAGE

The decision between using a rucksack or a suitcase is based on your travel style, comfort level and preference. Invest both time and money on finding the right piece, as backache or a collapsed bag would be disastrous. Many outdoor shops will fit a rucksack properly to your body and physicality: it is definitely not an item to order online.

USEFUL TIPS:

A waterproof cover – for protection in all weather
Multiple zips – for easily retrieving items inside
Padlocks – for safety (the more openings, the more padlocks required)
Adjustable straps – for a more personalised fit
Protective spine – for support

Four wheels – for stable manoeuvring
Hard case – for protection in all weather
Two separate pockets – for more efficient packing

Websites promote practical products, such as solar panel phone chargers. However, think about how extensively you will use them: the more packed, the heavier the weight that must be carried constantly around. From an unsettled stomach in Mumbai to altitude sickness in Chile, even at your weakest the bag should be light enough to manage.

Filter out the unnecessary.

Overpacking is a particularly common inconvenience, so think layers, especially if predicting considerable temperature changes. Items are hand-washable, so put travel wash on your packing list. Cheap clothing means effortless disposability, without sentimentality. Yet, consider your surroundings: if travelling in a deprived area, the local community will appreciate that supposedly useless t-shirt. Avoid insult by offering it sensitively though – or just leave it behind in your room.

Tops and Trousers

It is important to purchase clothing suitable for a region. Long-sleeved shirts and trousers are beneficial for both cultural and health reasons. In traditional societies, covering up retains modesty: religious sites cannot be visited with exposed knees and shoulders. Even in more liberal countries, t-shirts, rather than vest tops help travellers to blend in with locals and avoid unwanted attention. In jungles and humid areas, long clothing is also effective in protecting against mosquitos and other insects. This I learnt In Taiwan, where wearing shorts led to two hugely unpleasant spider bites. The swellings blistered and I was continually distracted because I was concerned about open wounds and infections. It was ironic, as I was in Asia; a continent famed for its markets full of light, inexpensive, cotton trousers. Never again will I let that happen to me!

Shoes

Include several pairs of walking shoes. Hiking boots and trainers need to be softened before travelling, or blisters will become your closest enemy. Only pack shoes that you will wear.

Outerwear

Entirely trip dependent, from cagoules to heavy coats to hats to scarves to gloves, the assessment will have informed you of a country's weather conditions. Buy all items from specialist outdoor shops, as the quality is designed specifically for travelling. Cagoules can be really sweaty though, so I usually pack an umbrella.

Multipurpose Items

In some communities, women must cover their head. I always pack a pashmina: a highly useful, easily hand-washable item that can be used as a head covering, scarf, blanket, towel or mat.

Intelligent packing makes life easier.

But I didn't think of that...

Over the years, several items have become prized possessions in my luggage:

1. **A CHEAP, OLD PHONE.** We forget that the most important function of a phone is to communicate. Packing a spare means staying in touch, no matter the situation.
2. **BUSINESS CARDS AND A RESUMÉ.** It always worth having printed contact details available to pass on to a possible future employer; remember a trip can produce the most unexpected outcomes.
3. **AN INFLATABLE CUSHION.** Those long bus journeys or night flights are uncomfortable, so any item that eases the journey is welcome! Create a bed by using alongside the pashmina blanket.
4. **A VARIETY OF BAGS.** During the average day, I carry an inexpensive, light, fold-up rucksack. In some

destinations, I avoid a bag completely. On these occasions, I hook a small purse (attached by a key-ring loop) to my bra strap.

5. **A SPARE WALLET**. This is for storing excess money in a safe.

B. HAND-LUGGAGE

Normally, I use a sturdy mid-sized rucksack (with multiple pockets), which has also been professionally fitted. This bag is ideal for overnight trips and more adventurous days out. In it I pack:

- **A CHARGER WITH A USB ATTACHMENT.** Journeys can be long, especially with flight delays, so a phone needs enough charge to reach the hotel. Add a replacement charger to luggage, just in case technology fails.
- **SPARE CLOTHES, ESPECIALLY UNDERWEAR.** It is more refreshing to arrive in a fresh outfit and sometimes luggage is lost.
- **PRINTED DOCUMENTS IN THE REQUIRED ORDER, INCLUDING PASSPORT**. Papers stored in chronological order creates efficiency and confidence. Organise in a brightly coloured folder, for effortless identification during the 'key item' check (passport, wallet, phone). Immigration can also refuse entry unless evidence of departure is produced, so this preparation is helpful.
- **MONEY.** Never put valuable items into your luggage.

Remember that at the end of the trip, you might need to pay for a taxi home, so retain some home currency.

- **HAND-SANITISER.** Consider cleanliness from the very beginning. Illnesses cause weakness; feeling strong is staying healthy.
- **EARPLUGS AND A FACE MASK.** Blocking both noise and light helps with sleeping.

TECHNOLOGY

In 2007, I vividly remember being shown Skype in an internet café in Brazil. When preparing for that trip, I never even considered packing my mobile because society was more frightened about theft than of a traveller not contacting home. How times have changed!

It now seems unfathomable to survive without a phone as its functions are endless: communication, diary, camera and bank account. Currently, most data plans for European customers include free roaming across the continent, but there is an expensive charge for the rest of the world. Although free public Wi-Fi networks are available, recent news reports suggest that they provide platforms for fraudulent activities, as passwords can be easily retrieved. Travellers therefore require other options.

SIM CARDS

A mobile can be unlocked, which means that the SIM works separately from the device. Ring your provider or visit a local phone shop for further assistance. By buying a SIM from the destination country, data can be utilised at a significantly lower cost than using a home plan abroad. Maps are then accessible in any place, and at any time, which is helpful for establishing location and routes. Pack your home SIM though, in case of emergencies.

APPS

Helpful apps assist with everything from finding restaurants to organising travel documents to creating a packing list. Prioritise the local taxi app, which is a different company for every region. It is worth setting up an account prior to arrival.

The increased reliance in communication has led to more ways of targeting the traveller. Dating apps have become popular, but using them is dangerous. Whilst abroad, our mindset is at its most liberal: we gain a sense of fearlessness. New friends encourage us to try new and exciting experiences; they re-tell stories of 'successes' and positive results. However, meeting up with complete strangers is never worth the risk. At home, we chat to real friends about dates, but on this trip, nobody important knows of our whereabouts.

So, if you really want to use the internet to socialise, use websites that charge for events.

SOCIAL MEDIA

Social media is useful for communicating with loved ones because one post informs multiple people simultaneously of your safety. This relieves the pressure of constantly contacting everyone individually, which is extremely time consuming. Friends and family also then feel more involved, as they are able to show an interest by leaving comments. The consequence: you understand that your community supports you and precious spare moments are spent talking to those who provide comfort or advice.

Prepare for a trip by setting up and sharing these pages, so that whilst away only the updates need completing.

TASK

So many areas need tackling. Ticking off sections
individually is challenging and multi-tasking is
inevitable. Remain organised by keeping notes.

Category	Item	Notes	Achieved
Documentation	Passport	*Expires in four months*	*Apply for a new passport*
	Visas		
	Travel Insurance		
	Money: – Cash – Cards		
	Printed booking confirmations		
	Printed itinerary		

Health	First aid kit
	Health appointments: – Travel nurse – Injections – Antimalaria tablets
	Mental health strategies
Packing	Luggage: – Backpack or suitcase – Clothing – Toiletries – Other
	Hand luggage
Technology	Telephone
	Apps
	Social Media
Other	

TRAVEL

The preparation is complete. The departure day is here. The trip commences.

The first week away is an overwhelming rollercoaster of emotion. First, there is relief that the plan is now a reality. This develops into some uncertainty and hesitation: everything around you is so shockingly different. Where is the familiarity, comfort and routine? For reassurance, you adopt an overconfident approach, which you think will help to 'prove yourself'. Then, a pride grows, especially when minor challenges are overcome.

On every trip, I cry. The pattern is always the same: tears fall straight after checking into the first hotel, having dragged my luggage upstairs and opened the bedroom door. I do feel released afterwards though.

Travelling solo is an achievement that should never be underestimated.

Social media, websites, blogs and apps all provide current and relevant information on the latest scams and advice associated with particular regions. Yet, over the years, I have discovered many tips of my own, no matter the travel style, comfort level or destination.

TIPS FOR JOURNEYS

With so many modes of transportation, whether it be an international or a domestic journey, it is important to:

1. **LEAVE ENOUGH TIME.** Reach an airport two hours before departure. Build transfer time into your schedule. Rush hours are different for every destination, so always seek advice.
2. **CHECK IN.** Use this two-hour waiting time for social media. Tagging yourself to an airport is a quick and easy way to inform everyone at home that you are well.
3. **PACK LUGGAGE METHODICALLY BEFOREHAND.** Pack essential items at the top of your case/backpack. For an evening arrival, prioritise pyjamas and a toothbrush, as you will be desperate for sleep after a long journey. For a day time arrival, pre-pack your day-bag, as rummaging around will inevitably take place in the accommodation lobby. Tidiness leads to efficiency, as in both situations, luggage needs immediately locking afterwards.
4. **KEEP POSSESSIONS IN SIGHT.** Pickpocketing on flights is becoming more widespread, as passengers are storing their bags behind eye line, rather than in

front. On days out, remember that a rucksack can be worn on the front, as well as the back.

5. **HOLD VALUABLES CLOSE.** Frequently check hand luggage for your passport, wallet and phone. Other belongings are more easily replaceable, so remain calm if you lose anything.

6. **EMBRACE THE VIEW OUT OF THE WINDOW.** An overprotective and defensive attitude creates an unconfident image. Instead, once luggage and valuables are secure, relax and admire that awe-inspiring scenery.

7. **AGREE A FARE BEFORE LEAVING.** With local taxis or tuk-tuks, barter at the beginning. Without a fixed rate, the driver has full control over the fee charged. Always use a metered cab.

8. **CARRY COINS.** To avoid being short-changed, never pay with a high value note, especially for taxis and ticket machines.

TIPS FOR DAYS AND NIGHTS OUT

Most destinations need exploring at all times of the day, so remember:

I. **CARRY ACCOMMODATION AND LOCAL EMERGENCY NUMBERS.** Sometimes a taxi driver is unable to locate your hotel or hostel. Having the number available allows them to ring reception to ask for directions.

2. **USE YOUR BRA.** Ladies, it can be your most trusted

friend! Situated in the most fortuitous place (underneath clothes and at the front), those two pockets provide safe storage. It is a sweaty location in hot and humid weather, so expect anything retrieved to be soaking wet, but things dry out quickly!

3. **WATCH PHONE USAGE.** It is tempting to post incredible sights instantaneously on social media, but holding a phone out in public makes you a target. Locals immediately identify you as a 'rich' tourist. This is an invitation for pickpockets; you cannot look at a screen and the surrounding environment.

4. **READ MAPS CAREFULLY.** Increasingly, we use our phones for map reading, so download or screenshot routes. In a street, never check your location by either opening a phone or a paper map. Instead, step inside the more private space of a shop or restaurant.

5. **GET LOST.** Take careful risks. Study maps over breakfast, and seek advice on areas to avoid, but then enjoy wandering the streets. Visit that shop, restaurant or café immediately though, as it will be impossible to find again!

6. **HOLD YOUR BAG AWAY FROM THE ROAD.** Theft from scooter drivers is becoming increasingly rife, particularly in South East Asia. Thieves grab a road-side bag – and take you with it.

7. **LOCK AWAY VALUABLES.** Use the accommodation safe. Secure all openings to luggage with padlocks. Take the minimum out with you during the day and evening.

8. **ABSORB ADVICE.** Locals provide excellent information, as they are a wealth of knowledge. Ask reception whether an area is safe to walk around in the evening. Heed the answer. In a high-standard bar or restaurant, employees can order a cab for you.

9. **BARTER!** Unlike Western culture, many societies expect price negotiation. Yet, consider the value of money: who would benefit more from that pound or dollar that you might save?

10. **BLEND IN.** Try not to stand out from the crowd. Expensive watches and jewellery are magnets for thieves.

11. **ACQUIRE A TIMETABLE.** If using local transportation, check return times. You do not want to be stranded away from accommodation.

12. **PUT THE CAMERA DOWN.** Life is for experiencing, not looking at through a lens. The memory is the live moment, not the video recorded.

13. **JUDGE PAYMENT CORRECTLY.** Nothing is free, whether it be the tour led by university students or the request for a picture. Keep coins available for those small hidden costs.

TIPS FOR FOOD AND DRINK

Water filtering standards abroad are inconsistent with our norm. Locals wash produce under the tap, so only **eat fruit and vegetables that can be peeled**, as the skin forms a protective barrier against impurities. **Refuse ice in all public bars and restaurants.** I resent the plastic wastage, but only **drink liquids, including alcohol, from sealed bottles or cans.**

Unfortunately, horror stories include barmen being paid to spike the drinks that they have poured. Indeed, bars and clubs can be unsafe for the solo traveller. For this reason, when travelling, I purchase drinks from a local supermarket. Safely back at accommodation, and sat by a pool or in reception, I can fully unwind. **Remember: heat, high-altitude and exhaustion also make the effects of alcohol unpredictable.**

Despite all the warnings about food and drink, **try new dishes!** I continue to dream about the passionfruit fish that I devoured in Hanoi in 2016. The restaurant was six floors up, and I sat outside admiring the incredible view of the lake and city. It was the hotel that had recommended this bargainous, yet memorable meal.

TIPS FOR FEELING LESS 'ALONE'

For me, loneliness is a rare occurrence. Usually, in a particular moment, I think fondly of how important people in my life would enjoy a place or experience too. Even so, there is regularly a craving for company. Sometimes, simply sitting silently in the presence of others is enough, but other times, there is a longing for conversation, as nobody has even spoken to you that day.

TO AVOID ISOLATION:

1. **SIT AT A BAR.** Be prepared to talk to anyone. Some people are wary and misconstrue friendliness, but many welcome you into their social group.
2. **CREATE A ROUTINE.** Staying in one location for several nights enables you to create a pattern, so eat breakfast at the same time, and in the same place, every day. By day three, faces become familiar and conversations begin more easily.
3. **SHARE TABLES AT RESTAURANTS AND CAFES.** In Asia, it is normal practice to dine with strangers. Occasionally, it is hard to find a common language, but everyone still tries to communicate. People are interesting and it is surprising who you can meet. Yet, do not fear sitting alone. I enjoy these moments: I put my phone away and I do not busy myself. I clearly remember my first visit to Melbourne in 2011. The waitress had wanted to sit me at the bar, despite the restaurant only being half-full. She had incorrectly judged me as embarrassed to be alone.

With so much advice, fear can become the overriding emotion. However, stand confident and let the trip design support you. Never forget that this world is full of hope and kindness, which is found in the most unexpected of places...

Kobe, the sixth largest city in Japan. I'd caught a local train, as I was attempting (and failing) to reach a spa town that was situated in the suburbs. Unfortunately, I had disembarked at the incorrect station. With English neither on the street signs, nor on the map in my hand, I was clueless as to my location. As a white, English woman with ash-blonde hair and blue eyes, it could not have been more obvious that I was a lost and helpless tourist. A lady stopped me. She spoke absolutely no English. Although she was in an obvious rush to head to work, she stood patiently in front of me, whilst I pointed at the map, trying to show her exactly where I wanted to reach. She began walking and signalled for me to follow. We soon arrived back at the station, where she then paid for my ticket and put me on the correct train. She even held her fingers up to indicate the number of stops that I needed to travel. Gut feeling had told me that she would help and I had accepted her kindness at face value. I will always remember her as the woman who made me feel less hopeless.

Another time, I was heading to Sydney to visit a close friend. I broke up the long journey from the UK in Hong Kong. After an exciting few days, I was ready to complete the final leg to Australia. I boarded the plane, which was already over an hour late, found my seat and readied myself for the night flight. Several hours later, we still hadn't taken off, finally being forced back into the terminal just after midnight. Thankfully, the day before, in a queue for an attraction, I had briefly met a friendly English couple, who happened to be taking the same flight. By 2 am, united in exhaustion, we created a plan: two would attempt to sleep, whilst the third would stay awake to watch the bags and every few hours, we would switch roles. It is completely absurd to trust strangers with your most precious valuables, but it seemed the right approach. Eighteen hours later, we eventually departed. I had been supported in a moment when I could have felt entirely alone.

It is these experiences that remain with you forever; they change your entire perspective of humanity. People are generous and can be trusted: not everyone is bad. So, take risk but trust and follow your instincts. Returning back to 'normal life' is challenging. Not everyone is interested in your personal journey – that increased confidence and improved outlook on life means that some people no longer understand you. Yet, your stories and successes of solo travelling are worth every sacrifice.

QUICK-FIRE QUESTIONS

HOW MUCH MONEY SHOULD I SAVE FOR A TRIP?

This depends on the length of the trip, comfort level and region. Your assessment should have answered this question. Save, save, save but never underestimate your total. It is always better to return home with money.

WHAT SHOULD I CARRY DURING THE DAY?

Usually, I put a full bottle of water, sunscreen, phone, hat and paper map into my fold-up backpack. A UV umbrella is handy for both rainy and sunny conditions. I also buy sweets, so I am ready for those low blood sugar moments, which are especially frequent in high altitude. I place some cash and my pre-paid travel money card into my bra. If valuable items are in my bag, then I wear it on my front.

Public toilets can be disgusting. The most memorable facility I came across was in Bolivia. Imagine this: a washing line of raw meat dangling over a hole in the desert floor. Needless to say, I refused the option. But pack tissues and hand-sanitiser for those unfortunate moments.

DO YOU EVER HATE A DESTINATION?

It can feel anticlimactic visiting a place, especially if it has been overphotographed. I refuse to spend money on a location I don't like, so I use the time to unwind instead. I find a café and watch the world go by.

DO YOU EVER FIND YOURSELF IN DIFFICULT SITUATIONS?

Yes! In Colombo, Sri Lanka, I was suddenly surrounded by three men, who were obviously working as a team: the first had a monkey on his shoulders; the second had a snake around his neck and the third man was trying to usher me into his tuk-tuk. Obviously, I felt very uneasy. I called out to a non-existent friend and confidently walked away.

> **IF SOMETHING IS UNCOMFORTABLE, THEN ESTABLISH AN ESCAPE ROUTEUTE – AND QUICKLY.**

I never worry about losing my possessions, as it is a complete waste of energy. If there is an emergency, contact your local embassy.

> **MY PARENTS ARE WORRIED ABOUT ME TRAVELLING ALONE. WHAT SHOULD I DO?**

The solo traveller cannot complete their journey without the love and support of family and friends. Their help will not make you a less capable and independent traveller, so include them in the planning stages.

Give them this guide, so together you realise that you can achieve absolutely everything.

FOR MORE INFORMATION:

Follow: PlanSafeTravel (Twitter)
and plansafetravel (Instagram)

Visit: www.plansafetravel.com